EQUIVOCAL

EQUIVOCAL

JULIE CARR

ALICE JAMES BOOKS

FARMINGTON, MAINE

10 9 8 7 6 5 4 3 2 1

Alice James Books are published by Alice James Poetry Cooperative, Inc.,
an affiliate of the University of Maine at Farmington.

ALICE JAMES BOOKS
238 MAIN STREET
FARMINGTON, ME 04938

www.alicejamesbooks.org

Library of Congress Cataloging-in-Publication Data
Carr, Julie,
Equivocal / Julie Carr.
p. cm.
Poems.
ISBN-13: 978-1-882295-63-0
ISBN-10: 1-882295-63-3
I. Title.

PS3603.A77425E68 2007
813'.6--DC22
2007010857

Alice James Books gratefully acknowledges support from the University of
Maine at Farmington and the National Endowment for the Arts. ❦

Cover Art: Alphabet blocks in the cover photograph are artworks
by Elizabeth Lewis, joyofart@peoplepc.com. Photograph by Steve Carr.

Occasional lines in "Wrought" are borrowed or adulterated from Stanley
Cavell, *Emerson's Transcendental Etudes* (Stanford University Press, 2003).

The untitled lyrics in "Letter Box" were made with the help of a series of quar-
ter-inch cubes (as pictured on the cover) constructed by the artist Elizabeth
Lewis. Each cube is painted on four sides with one of the letters of the alpha-
bet; the other two sides bear an image of an object that begins with that let-
ter. Q: queen and question mark. M: moon, Marilyn Monroe. Flag and a foot,
grapes and a golfer, Abe Lincoln and a leaf. There are ten cubes from numbers
0 to 9.

ACKNOWLEDGMENTS

GRATEFUL ACKNOWLEDGMENT to the editors of the following journals in which some of these poems first appeared: *Bayou, Boston Review, Columbia Poetry Review, Denver Quarterly, Five Fingers Review, The Iowa Review, Parthenon West Review, Pool, Tarpaulin Sky, Verse,* and *Xantippe.*

Thanks to Heather McHugh and David Lehman for including "Marriage" in *The Best American Poetry 2007.* Thanks also to Rebecca Wolff and Catherine Wagner for including "Wrought History," "Time Paper," and "Iliadic Familias (with insertions from Homer)" in *Not for Mothers Only: Contemporary Poems on Child-Getting and Child-Rearing* (Fence Books, 2007), and to Nancy Kuhl of Phylum Press for printing "Wrought Sonnet Rain" and "Mirage" as limited edition broadsides.

Thank you Matthew Cooperman, Shira Dentz, Jessica Fisher, Lyn Hejinian, Rusty Morrison, Linda Norton, Margaret Ronda, Peter Streckfus, and Liz Young for your friendship, reading, and writing. Thanks especially and always to Tim Roberts. Much gratitude also to Elizabeth Lewis for the use of her artwork, and to Steve Carr for his photography. This book is for Carolyn Grace and Alice Roberts.

CONTENTS

WROUGHT

LETTER BOX

ELEVEN ODES

EQUIVOCAL

The quiet circle in which Change and Permanence co-exist, not by combination or juxtaposition, but by an absolute annihilation of difference / column of smoke, the fountains before St. Peter's, waterfalls / God!—change without loss—change by perpetual growth, that [at] once constitutes and annihilates change. The past, & the future included in the Present // oh! it is awful.

—S. T. Coleridge

WROUGHT

1.

Virtue is a kind of foot

Since the lip of the girl, our girl, does not yet contain dying

Once a wall of peaches drew my eye and stood me to—

Trod, have trod, have trod.

2. Wrought Gerund

Sick child in his parents' bed making the plastic things talk.

Arrive thinking: I mean to leave everything I say as fallen.

Moving a leaf with my foot.

> redeem the surrogate goodbyes
> the sheet a stream in your hand

> Beckett

Standing in a field: Violence to the voice of Nature
moving quickly like spit.

Gerund: from *gerundus* or *gerere*—
to bear, to carry on.

3. Wrought Pledge

I'll not criticize the aged.
I'll not worry you with my health problems.
Not crowd you in the kitchen.
Not recklessly spend.
I'll not shovel over the grave-markers.
Not stand roadside weeping.
I'll not pour salt into my eyes.
If cruelty is the end of thinking and thinking the end of cruelty,
I'll not pride myself in thinking I am thinking.

He flosses her teeth for her. She worries it will hurt,
that she'll go bankrupt, that her family will disown her.
Are there places for people like her? Will he cut her mouth?

Each day needs are met: Dissonance, insight,
the woman at the station, the great man, the impressionable man,
the silent man. Already there is the father and the other father,
the man with heels, the man in the tub, the man tunneling
through waste, the man opening his heart to the gunner. Already
the man falling into a haze or falling into a courtyard
pool in Fort D., already the man without lips,
the man without fingers, the man without money, the man without
children, the man keeping a beat beneath the body of a plane.

What prepares me for this particular pain—
the pain of leaving things as they are—
of taking them as they are?

This, the condition of breathing, of rot.

4. Time Paper

Why does the philosopher call the *time of the now*
        the *technical expression of messianic time?*

What use the word "technical"?

Turns to face me, but its features are transparent,
        empty as a spill of foam.

My boy walks—almost steps on—the carcass of a bird.

      ◆

I grieve that grief can teach me nothing: Emerson,
        choosing tautology to reveal emptiness.

To think is to describe with indifference: feasters on a holiday
        in any country, the breath as it freezes

        just beyond the mouth.

Fallen leaf: one side pure black, the other yellow as a
        feline eye.

Oh, continent less imagined: manhood begins in the womb.

      ◆

I am nothing, writes Pessoa, I am the extended commentary
        on a book that doesn't exist.

In the center of me is a vortex like the crawlspace
        in a house never built.

The morning comes according to its numbers, which means it is
        safe to rise.

The family that shares my DNA, my name, and in some cases
my memory, is getting out of bed, peeing, putting on slippers,

walking out for the paper, beginning to play.

Emerson says the private thought is the universal
        but it must never be construed as the universal

lest we kill its difference.

She's made the bed, stretching the sheet over the blankets,
        which doesn't work. She errs not because unable
        to hear the spectacle of humankind's oblivion,

but because time and its order is not.

"Technique" from Latin *texere* means "to weave."

The tapestry of now is endless,

        would be another way to translate the philosopher.

The child walks upstairs on all fours like a cat.

5. Wrought History

In the history of the child there is always an account of her
        beginning, and she knows herself to be magnified
        by the tale.

Gathering the stones into a circle, each one turned inward
        as if they have faces.

She walks through the zoo with notebook and pencil
        like a reporter from *The New York Times*.

Like other mothers, I say no to desserts, noise, and spitting,
        but I am not a mother and I am not
        like anyone else.

I and a prairie dog meet "in person."

In the rental car she says, *I like rental cars.*
        We should buy a rental car. If we clean our car,
        we will have a rental car.

I speak exactly as everyone else speaks; fall asleep exactly
        as anyone else falls asleep.

There is no greater expression of pride than to refer to oneself
        as nothing, no greater claim for one's centrality
        than the claim that one has none.

It was raining, I tell her again, a man drilling a hole
        into the avenue below.

6. Wrought Memory

Yellow kickball soars over ballwall.

Boyish girl, long shorts, short *ha!* throws her head laughing
upward—her girlish girlfriend,

gaze away.

He cartwheeled on maroon carpet beyond tanks of lobsters,
rubber-banded claws.

Daylight twists through honeysuckle leaves to the chair where I
read, incapable of sensing an end.

Lipwidth mispellings indicate the futureless self.

Transparent embarrassment lifted him to his feet
while a room of adults regret laughing.

I've never had such fun as with you, says my mother.

My four-year-old girl approves birthday decor:
You're a good one. A good decorator. A good mother.

Private griefs become public when theorized: I cannot get it
nearer me.

I look up now: *For what is bounded by the now is thought
to be time:* Aristotle.

Birth of a girl. Crossed my knees.

Autumn: she plunged into the river Lethe: No, no, go not thou.

7. Wrought Sonnet Rain

Bodily
pain woke me to poor
Miss Finch's
delicate face and curious
hand.

You are the owner
of one complete
heart. Cup
of rain

on the deck would like lake,
torrent, or current—
cupped beloved's
voice in my mouth.
I am an idle visitor.

8. Envy Song

Rain excuses lassitude and Game Boy.
Fells fronds and rusts bolts.

So my maker, the only way to echo you is to echo you.
As when in sex we mimic the breath of the other.
It's a kind of pouring, a fraught stream
of envy and noise.

Rapt: holding ash in my face like a woman just emerging
        from a house where someone's died.
It was beautiful becoming female stashing blood in a game
        nobody played.

I was remnant of a sonnet, of the gap before the couplet,
jumping woodside in *full-throated ease*.

LETTER BOX

A tree looks
like the letter T

       which is what it represents.

The moon appears to be backward

               but only mimics a cat.

The duck might be talking on the phone
and will have to be turned over.

       I've decided to remove the king
       but doing this leaves a hole I cannot fill.

Examining the hole with my finger disrupts the painting

       and now within, the characters weep.

The heart bordered by black appears as a planet,

as a horse galloping over the sun.

Go: the singing feet. But there's nowhere
to land (my fisted hands).

Seen from beneath, mine will be a flag. It,
the galloping,

blossoms.

I woke as a pair of arrows, a yo-yo owl, guarding my flag

with my five, my two threes, my seven. I, loving God

by laying eggs for my country——a rainbow-striped zebra

or a black and white zebra or just a Z——

woke with the clock on my breast like a rose.

I'd been dancing in red shoes as an empty box meaning nothing.

All of this says, *I longed for you*——the ghost of a tree, the teacher.

LETTER

This is how I make it: with my hands, like a cake. Since the clock's stopped, I must have been sleeping. Slowly every book is removed from the shelf, every bird makes a morning tune. The freeway is full of what was and isn't. We call that commute. I've never been so angry in all my life. That is why I smile so readily.

Once I was opening a door for my son and as he skipped through—back leg bent up, head thrown back, yellow gun tucked into his sleeve—I was aware I had just left my happiest moment. Everything I read that year engaged the non sequitur as glee, insincerity, or resistance. I decided to turn such devices to my own uses. Tucked in but triggerless, they'll form one out of anything: stick, soap, sandwich.

Dreamt at the chalkboard, our manager concludes his plan. We're to write it down, but not all of us are convinced of his authority. And yet, not convinced of our own. Finally, the food arrives and that solves it, as when, during the most intensely terrifying arguments on the congressional floor, someone makes a joke. *Excuse me,* the joke begins.

Outside then. The children complain: *We always go hiking!* To quiet them I tell again of the wizard who will turn you into the thing you love. My son becomes a jar of maple syrup and pours himself all down my daughter, who has become a slide. Luckily, their friend Miriam is water and cleans them up. In the logic of becoming unmade I make myself a mother.

It's almost done. I must look for epigraphs while the muted clock keeps me company in a room where leaves strewn across the floor mean I've come through a garden to find the name of love, the definition of a maker:

But I was a lover, another thought began, sliding over the other silently and orderly as fish not impeding each other.

The fog is in. I cut down many branches of the tree. Red blouse under white box. The calendar folds. Was I an O? A king with a golden crown? Was I, will I be, fun?

Volcanic fire in the face of the queen.
One eye toward myself, the other natal, removed.

From zero to one I look for food.

I am lost in your face,
or under it.

This can't be the queen, she's too close to the duck!
We put her in the corner; she eyes us from there.
Her crown and her veil disguise her youth.
Sweet turtle, she whispers, painting a leaf by a moon,
why am I surrounded?

The zero-eye—

      a rising balloon.

The cat, owl, mouse:
set in a scene of murderous hunger.

But if each event can be reversed
the scenes of childhood become mere sound-effects—

         a flag ripples, a bush rustles,
         we can't remember

         the words for anything at all
         and begin to cry.

LETTER 2

Three dancers in the park roll their T-shirts to their ribs,
flip onto their hands.

Have you noticed how common handstands have become?
I've been weeping, but not so anyone could tell. An *S* in the
center of my form flush with the fire from my neighbor's
smoke. A blister on my finger foreshadows the shattered
taillight. Hold still, duck, we wish to watch your feathers
dry. My children climb the fence to talk to the pigs.
I am that: steadying.

There are two kinds of makers.
One's a master, the other's a must.

Here's the absolute truth you were looking for: I know the
ground by my feet on it, know my mind by your distance
from it. And may all things bear a new name

in the rush of becoming unknown. I dreamt my book
was written in marker, with glued in photos of women
and cars.

The children dump the letters out. The children put the letters
in. Then I take the letters away (they are beginning to fight).
It's a toy, I say, but a grownup one.

Loiter in the car-lot tending the silence. Light bounces
a rubber doll.

A ferry immobilized in thickening ice. *Equivalence
undone leads to correspondence.*

Cartoon skeletons, an inverted I.
Bowler seeking mind: the flat joke.

Two eggs broken with a device meant to save.

The being was only a boat, though it knew its way back home.

The hat flew off and hid itself under a bush.
I found it and set it on its head.

The arrow points downward
which is why she can't figure out where to go.

I remind her that downward means forward,
but admit it's a bit odd.

At her back, a series of questions she isn't asking.
When did dinosaurs become dancers?

We hiked a hill that wasn't really beautiful.
We made the kids compete, which turned out badly.

If the mother does not eat
they stand her on her head.

The sward is dark—footsteps in crushed wet grass.

And now, back to town!

LETTER 3

I am the grass and the budding
instrumental.

I the sand sacrificial
eraser.

The large dog pushes
the smaller off the cliff, and I am

        the hiding from death.

And you—
my heaviness, my rearing-up, my having nothing

                  to say.

LETTER 4

A mother in third person does not easily make sense.
On the organic telephone, in my sentient email, I hold
formally to her love. I sleep suddenly in my book. In my
free heart my presence flings a look at my past.
Excuse me, dear honored, dear photographed, bodily,
I believe myself to have been framed.

I wanted to watch the mind, but *a* mind is not *the* mind,
it's a road drawn in pencil on a postcard saying *follow*
to a bent over, a falling over, tree. April: a tunneled train.
I'm taking time off.

Patience, hard thing! Hopkins over again, and I feel thy
finger and find thee. Alice pointing saying, I've done this,
I've written my name and only once did I misspell it.
Lips and eyes liquefy. We wander up and down the paths:
succulent and cacti, azalea and rose. I'm misspelling too.

Dark descending, and most art merciful then. Says Alice,
Let's play meeting. She wants a poem-meeting
and puts her head down in the dirt to find it.

                               Dealing in pleasure,
my mothering—

My friend's children climb the signpost with their
monkey-feet. To keep myself, I invite them in. The water
boils and I put whatever in it. It's easy to spoon out Jell-O
so no one day is too dark. My friend arrives to retrieve
them and peels one off my son. To keep the voice secondary
to what comes of the hand.

Presently, we found a hat.
But there was no head.

The news beckoned like a duck circling bread.
We allowed ourselves to be surrounded,

although we could still look upward.

Two rising suns,
too red, determined

eyes brushed

sideways to light
upon hilt

of my own
son, wrecking the saving

device while
singing while

mine.

Geometric aged paintings
balance my wan excessive you.

Unknown buffoon, my rose:

in your center, the arrow pointing down.

The fog's lift gives us this "view from above"
from which we discuss

the privilege of love.

The unmanifested face was my mother's and I kissed it.
She was very near phobic so we kept things quiet.

Slipping a pencil into my mouth I wrote on my tongue:
      loved, unloved.

The eye-bolt: a silence as empty as a flash of perfect distance.

ELEVEN ODES

And in regenerate rapture turns my face
Upon the devious coverts of dismay

—D.G. ROSSETTI

Ravel

The murmur in my wedding ring

like loose talk surrounds this unlacing. Bobbins
make turns, fingers miss. Slower then.

     ♦

                          Molten-hot

breasts—growing matter.

I've thought to cry, reaching to
                     salt us.

     ♦

Fever happening in the fold. That plan
wrapping us in its shallow crime—

the frailest wool-omen-thread.

Waves

Ghostly
    sea-flaws,   formerly rows,

the earlier vows,
                like flashes of fashion,

flit skyward.

     ◆

                I think about

a lot less.

     ◆

When he gathered the mussel shells

they were studded with barnacles—
    wedding cakes.

                      I stood aside.

What over-passed me?

Sand

You face the grain
while the lace-leaded sea reaps waves.

                Shift your eyes.

There's too much sun.
                Lines, softer lines, softer chill.

    ♦

    Miles sit within blue

                as this sand, sea-calmed,

waits for that swill, that ode.

    ♦

You're blazoned. And still
in the slight veiling your body does.

You were tending in, lightly startled.

Now stand, unwilling to move.

Fidelity

The sea mends with its minnowed lace
and remains untraceable like a living face.

Sand in the mouth
         from the dream's rushing force.

And my hand

        tossing hot slate, hot
        shivers of law.

Sow

Someone dug up my flowers.

But that was me.
To redeem demanded mending

the flaws in the dirt.

         ◆

Noon-green trees would shade the wreck I'd planted.
Rocking, they shimmered,

merging where rougher winds shoved.

I shoveled over the ripped surface
until even my face, sewn as bad news.

Will

In rain, with knees like water,
our son falls.

Another child soon—
and a wild chill swells

    the walls and shutters

            both mind and matter

      ◆

for the moment lies intact where we will.

Mirage

I forgot your face.
But it wasn't your face.

♦

Leaves
       video the sky:

the sun's
       verdant memory. An eye

felt as ravine.

Reap

Make her body. Keep sake.

Rapture softer am.

                The baby lies compromised.
                          Dark core donates space.

  Yet some touch,
  some break,
  something.

Then, rooms as shared lake.

                And she turns,
                    sure

            to live here—
          form in hand.

Excess

She swings a wild heliotrope up into our sight.

Pop tunes bloom in the roar of noon.

Our fingertips only skin deep

skim her least hid ways.

The baby's moves find mind's keener ends:

keen, keen, keen.

Dim moon in its own park plays.

Our lowered orbs in her twined strands

steal her eye-arcs.

Enfant Gâté

You skitter finally—
          such a bird's gait.

Lulled through dark's gate you must
                         scatter self.

You're somewhere full or
          nowhere.   Furled leaves

the new wet webs
               catching your great green

breath. There's trouble
          somewhere   full

trouble.

The fool of sleep humming

and our hanging onto
               scribing more into your eyes.

All girls are felled.

But I could not gather you with what I read

          not glean in you

what it said. *I called not to you to one eye red* not kid

       rib or bribe it

       to describe the crib or cry

not add you or lure you—

The world is water.

Marriage

On edge

and on——

whether manna or nominal

I can't quite keep

a noun in the mouth.

Avid. Avidly

bare prayer came

forcing itself down

from your foot, my foot, my hand.

Formal yet mannered yet

lavished and lain

and I measure

allegiance

as leisure is rain.

EQUIVOCAL

There is no other truth than a statistical one.

—SIMONE DE BEAUVOIR

Rake (creation)

I.

My son kisses me until I turn my face his way.
The eucalyptus hills adore us;
we open them with our feet.
This, the shape of the poem I will write
the child I did not make:

So soon
sped through   But these are not the words.
this earth

II.

So soon
the hand made
useful, raked
into furrows not its own.

Saturation

And each time she rose to begin a rain was falling on the leaves outside, and as the leaves shook in the slight wind they released the water to their roots, and so my mother dipped her hands into the pot of cooling dye to grab swaths of wet wool, to sling the wool over the line. Then, pouring honey from the large jar to the smaller meant keeping the pouring arm still while tilting the mouth of the small one toward the pouring.

This was the interruption anticipated: to turn one's attention to the desire of another. (*Gull chicks, silvery.*) The saturated world. But if tedium is fabricated, why the urge to close the mouth, to stop the kiss? I've never yet measured the breadth of my love: like a balloon slowly giving out its helium, it rests soft, deflated, two feet from the floor. Sensing or announcing: this was my best performance ever.

People, listeners, mythology grows back.

Rebirth bears its roots into the hearts of the governed.

While that tree parties, almost butterfly,

our flag slaps dead concentration.

◆

My dancers, my knock-knock jokers,

to do it they've done it they're done.

In debt or in doubt we cull the world's muscle,

fear no vernacular. This

maximum trial, this bleaker swale.

Iliadic Familias (with insertions from Homer)

My mother used to cry in the car while driving. This was terrifying to me in the back seat. Not only was she responsible for my safety, but I could not see her face. And now I cry in the car while driving. My children behind me fight over who gets to hold the twist-tie. This is a particularly deadly fight. I turn the news up so as not to hear them. I want to hear the mother who is talking about her dead son so that I can cry. Sometimes they ask me why I am crying. I always say, *The war*. This is how they come to be against the war. It is also how I came to be against the war that made my mother cry. She used to say, *It was not politics that got to me. What did I care about politics? It was thinking about the neighbor's son*. This is the famous fierceness of mothers. We do not want to listen to our children fighting because it will distract us from the war, which is making us cry. One mother says she opens the newspaper and immediately begins to cry, even before she reads anything. Another cannot watch child-in-danger movies. This is also true for me to an extreme degree. Once I was up half the night worrying for a girl in a movie who'd had her appendix out. The surgery was placed in the plot in order to bring her uncle and his boyfriend back together. Their mutual concern and love for the girl was a sign of their continued love for each other. This I knew. I also knew, incidentally, that it was fiction. However, I could not sleep because they never showed the girl back home. In the final shot she was asleep in the hospital bed. We were meant to be thinking about the two men who loved each other, who were watching over her as if she were *their* child, to be thinking about love and how it is not the exclusive property of parents or heterosexuals, but belongs to everybody. But I wanted the girl to wake up. In the morning, I told my husband and he was furious with me. He wants me to be able to watch movies and it is more and more evident that I can no longer watch movies. This, according to my husband, is a pathetic failure to be objective, rational, and to have fun.

II.

My mother used to cry in the car while driving to stop the sorrowful fighting. This was terrifying to me in the back seat. We shall fight again afterward, until the divinity chooses between us. Not only is she responsible for my safety, she gives victory to one or the other. And now I cry in the car while driving. By this time the terms of death hang over us. My children behind me fight. There is no sparing time for the bodies of the perished; this is a particularly deadly fight. Standing there in their midst, I turn the news up high. Now the sun, rising out of the quiet water and the deep stream of the ocean speaks of the mother who is speaking about her dead. As they wept warm tears they lifted them. Sometimes they ask me who I am crying. In the same way, on the other side, their hearts in sorrow. She used to say, *It was not politics, what did I care about politics? Is there any mortal left on the wide earth who will still declare to the immortals his mind and its purpose?* This is the famous fierceness of mothers. We do not want to listen to these children because it will distract us from what makes us. There is little breathing space in fighting. This is also true for me to an extreme degree. My desire has been dealt with roughly. Their mutual concern and love for her was a sign of their love for each other. Said one to the other: *Obey to the end this word I put upon your attention so that you can win, for me, the lovely girl.* But they never showed the girl back home. Tell me now, you Muses, how fire was first thrown. We were meant to be thinking of love as property, but wanting the girl to wake up, I never did. Drinking from a spring of dark running water, willing her to wake, in the heart of each one was a spirit untremulous, and he wants me to watch, he is furious. Your mother nursed you on gall! You have no pity! This is a failure to be. You would gather in groups to have fun, to be rational, yet the desire in your heart is to watch the grim encounter.

III.

My mother, an unearthly noise, I could not see her face, as wolves
make havoc among lambs over who gets to hold the black earth,
burdened, so as not to hear them, by the works of men, I turned
to the neighbor's son huddled inside his movie, he in the dust face
downward was also true for me, mouth open to the bright spear,
willing him to wake, the heart in my breast was balanced, be-
tween two ways, was pathetic, as if he were *my* child, as if where
the beating is enclosed in the arch of the muscle is a failure to ra-
tion, to be, a lowing bell, a bellowing.

Equivocal

If the herb in my mouth and the grout in the wall
rot as the wail wells over

will the sore on my hand, the bush that I've cut

heal in daylight's cover?

Foreclosure

Stealthily, a cold dream leaves the scene to be described
      by someone else. I am not

a fiction writer. But I've got my book, and I know
      what this means,

my book soaked in blood. Not *my* blood, but it's the measure
      of my heartlessness.

To have heart I must be still and take what dies into me.

My boy awake

gathers words for their tunnels. We call to him,
but he's not here, he's scanning the walls for signs.

To be heated I must remain thrilled

and replace my eyes willingly. I was marrying, and the train came
bringing the mythic wedding members. I slipped unseen

under the ocean and waited through silence

to be found or to be foreclosed.

The brain's high note. The blood's.

The last foot of thought from out of sleep

skipped. My hand to a switch it's just past six

borrowed the sound sound of the railing, white in the white

of the air, and spoke up the house like the vine, in the darker

part of the light, where is my book?

On the blue-blanched highways of the west

in the waist-high sulfur-rich bubbles in the cliff rock

whose pine is this? The holiday thrust

begins on this coast as this white railing singes

as sun. To birch like that. To house.

Single story pastel burrow, furrows of garlic-rich soil:

where is a word? I've said "abide,"

used what was given: the heat and the threat of the sun.

Equivocal

If that bird in my hand and that bear in the trees
were to read what I store in the crease of my eye,

if the green infant shoots and the blond bomb blooms
in the garden we measured with the width of our arms,

in the gate-guarded seed-spill we plotted and pooled

might nativity carry our cure?

House / Boat

Broad, the river belled in a thud of sun.

I climbed aboard, I rowed. A border flew open like a cough.
I leaned back to balance

my oars as they dipped
to green and red furrows of light.

My boat rocked, steady, un-steady.
Was I welcomed? It seemed I was as I gripped

and privately beheld.

The night soon lost its head.
Pulling up now, parking,

looking for something to eat,
to redeem.

The wind shook the seedpod but the seedpod
wasn't moved.

And though I thought I'd done the damage I was born for,

there was still so much to step through,
so much to mar.

Equivocal

If the cock pecks at glass and the glass frames a face
in the underfed city of overbuilt transit,

might I claim for my comfort the effort to picture
your face in the glass, your transitioning eye?

If I draw from my ear a rose made of chiming
or hold in my mouth a bird made of cream,

if I place in your hand the flavor of typing
or lay on your lap the sound of my name?

The emptying parking lot, the tube of hair gel, the unmade bed,

this drop of sauce on my sleeve,

I understand what they mean. For thus, by ordinary actions
and without attracting attention,

I can cut some of the roots of the tree.

He tells me she's studying Italian. This is disquieting
as English is now so troublesome.

The scent of dirt in front of my house,
shade and ivy-covered earth: the work of a generation.

I knew just what he wanted but didn't respond—
this is the problem of the mind.

My mother seeing snow says the snow is scared, or scarred,
by the shadows of alders.

But what now the status of the root?

Tocqueville: *A despot usually forgives his subjects*
       for not loving him,

provided they do not love one another.

In a culture of life, if I dream we make love,
       do I spend the day gratified,

having gratified him?

The onion, after all, is chopped up and fried.

Standing on a rock he saw the wave coming and turned his back
       in defense.

It swept over him, knocking him off to sprawl in the sand.

I missed this entirely, looking up to find him livid and wet.

The face: kissed and peered into remains an arrangement.

Gaze at an ordinary object, I instruct my children,
let's see if it transforms before your eyes

       into a portal to the eternal.

Equivocal

If I pour from my hat all the water in Venice
and spread out my fingers to show I am true,

if I drag from my basement the boxes of boxes

boxes of broken, the boxes of strewn

If I pay for your tailor to tear out the lining,

to cut out the pockets of your most-loved coat,
then pay him again to line it with bees' wings,

to sew to the pockets the bladders of pigs

If you call through the dark the name of your savior,
a three-year-old goddess with wings made of paper,

and I run down the meadow of fish bones and sheep's wool

to throw myself into the vale of my girlhood

will you then be enraptured?

Song in Two Parts

When the toys grow wings
and the walls absorb the moisture of bodies
I hide myself in my cells—becoming organic

Burying my ancestry requires so little
I've lost touch with other mothers,

lost touch with my sex

Across the table she rests her face on her fist—

my baby has hurt her foot

To write this, a kind of penance—something else

for the hand to do—and is there a reason to stop
writing: she has hurt her foot?

◆

Here where the toys take flight or fall sleeping under rags,
the stars at the whir of the wires start—I am beginning

to think as swelling
roses splay

Equivocal

If I move from my chair to stand at the breaking
stand in the falling sound of the caller

If I wake in the early dark of the near-day,
tear from the garden all growth unbidden

If the snail on the glass slides unheeded skyward,
the flies in the corner cluster unbothered

If I promise to carry the water, the sweaters,
the small bits of stories that fracture and crease

If I promise to mend them or hide them or tell them
as you would have told them if you'd been untroubled

If I glue to my back your plans for tomorrow
or pin to your soles the map of your city

If I sew to your eyes the scenes of your bedroom
and tie to your hands the hands of the others

If I fly to your bedroom or burn in the garden,
cluster like glue in the sounds of your tongue

If I carry your face as an untroubled day
while blood-like the water breaks meaning to fractions

If mending your eyes means boiling my soles
and cities grow others skyward unheeded

If dark waking early hides plans in its clothes,
the hand that is bitten holds promise tight-fisted

If the batting of eyes, the bursting of sides,
the boiling of blood, and the burning face

If the torn-out heart, the bitten tongue,
the hands made of thumbs, the belly of flies

If water, if mother, if nail, if thumb,
if blood, or mouth, or mind, or none, then none.

Weather swinging in or up, my breath holding nothing,
        the widening is

Appetite measurement, waterfall symposium, let the letters leak

A fish hangs by its mouth by its more specific lip

Terrific, they hurled themselves against the wall and leapt
        from the tops of trees

My education, a corona, then an anchor, sample Moses
        on my shoulder

I'm not really into science right now; wood seen through water
water seen through glass, invents me

Candor of doorway, swung and banging

If complacent, more at please, more at flood, more at floored

Or weeding with the outsider's desire to come in

Vibration of the sacrificial
leaf in its spin

The day unlike the hose, lit as if to burn, wound upon itself,
is like my hand, purposive

as doubled tripled seconds, living or lit

into one into one

Recent Titles from Alice James Books

A Thief of Strings, Donald Revell
Take What You Want, Henrietta Goodman
The Glass Age, Cole Swensen
The Case Against Happiness, Jean-Paul Pecqueur
Ruin, Cynthia Cruz
Forth A Raven, Christina Davis
The Pitch, Tom Thompson
Landscapes I & II, Lesle Lewis
Here, Bullet, Brian Turner
The Far Mosque, Kazim Ali
Gloryland, Anne Marie Macari
Polar, Dobby Gibson
Pennyweight Windows: New & Selected Poems, Donald Revell
Matadora, Sarah Gambito
In the Ghost-House Acquainted, Kevin Goodan
The Devotion Field, Claudia Keelan
Into Perfect Spheres Such Holes Are Pierced, Catherine Barnett
Goest, Cole Swensen
Night of a Thousand Blossoms, Frank X. Gaspar
Mister Goodbye Easter Island, Jon Woodward
The Devil's Garden, Adrian Matejka
The Wind, Master Cherry, the Wind, Larissa Szporluk
North True South Bright, Dan Beachy-Quick
My Mojave, Donald Revell
Granted, Mary Szybist
Sails the Wind Left Behind, Alessandra Lynch
Sea Gate, Jocelyn Emerson
An Ordinary Day, Xue Di
The Captain Lands in Paradise, Sarah Manguso
Ladder Music, Ellen Doré Watson
Pity the Bathtub Its Forced Embrace of the Human Form, Matthea Harvey
The Arrival of the Future, B.H. Fairchild
The Art of the Lathe, B.H. Fairchild

Alice James Books has been publishing exclusively poetry since 1973. One of the few presses in the country that is run collectively, the cooperative selects manuscripts for publication through both regional and national annual competitions. New regional authors become active members of the cooperative, participating in the editorial decisions of the press. The press, which historically has placed an emphasis on publishing women poets, was named for Alice James, sister of William and Henry, whose fine journal and gift for writing went unrecognized within her lifetime.

TYPESET AND DESIGNED BY DEDE CUMMINGS

PRINTED BY THOMSON-SHORE
ON 50% POSTCONSUMER RECYCLED PAPER
PROCESSED CHLORINE-FREE